BEAUTIFUL BIOMES

GRASSLAND BIOME

by Elizabeth Andrews

Cody Koala
An Imprint of Pop!
popbooksonline.com

abdobooks.com
Published by Pop!, a division of ABDO, PO Box 398166, Minneapolis, Minnesota 55439. Copyright ©2022 by Abdo Consulting Group, Inc. International copyrights reserved in all countries. No part of this book may be reproduced in any form without written permission from the publisher. Cody Koala™ is a trademark and logo of Pop!.

Printed in the United States of America, North Mankato, Minnesota

102021
012022

THIS BOOK CONTAINS RECYCLED MATERIALS

Cover Photo: Lubo Ivanko/Getty Images
Interior Photos: Shutterstock Images, 1, 5 (top, bottom left), 6–7, 9, 10, 13, 14, 16–17, 18–19, 20; deimagine/Getty Images, 5 (bottom center)

Editor: Tyler Gieseke
Series Designer: Laura Graphenteen

Library of Congress Control Number: 2021942246

Publisher's Cataloging-in-Publication Data
Names: Andrews, Elizabeth, author.
Title: Grassland biome / by Elizabeth Andrews
Description: Minneapolis, Minnesota : Pop!, 2022 | Series: Beautiful biomes | Includes online resources and index.
Identifiers: ISBN 9781098241032 (lib. bdg.) | ISBN 9781098241735 (ebook)
Subjects: LCSH: Grasslands--Juvenile literature. | Biotic communities--Juvenile literature. | Habitats--Juvenile literature. | Life zones--Juvenile literature. | Grassland animals--Juvenile literature. | Grassland plants--Juvenile literature. | Grassland ecology--Juvenile literature.
Classification: DDC 577.4--dc23

Hello! My name is
Cody Koala

Pop open this book and you'll find QR codes like this one, loaded with information, so you can learn even more!

Scan this code* and others like it while you read, or visit the website below to make this book pop.

popbooksonline.com/grassland-biome

*Scanning QR codes requires a web-enabled smart device with a QR code reader app and a camera.

Table of Contents

Chapter 1
Grassy Plains 4

Chapter 2
Types of Grasslands 8

Chapter 3
Grassland Plants 12

Chapter 4
Grassland Animals 18

Making Connections 22
Glossary 23
Index 24
Online Resources 24

Chapter 1

Grassy Plains

A biome is a large, natural area. It is known for the plants and animals that live there, and its **climate**.

grassland

desert

freshwater

Watch a video here!

A plain is a large, flat area with few trees.

Grasslands are biomes that are covered mostly by grasses. They get the perfect amount of rain for

these plants to grow. There is not enough **precipitation** for larger plants like trees to grow.

Chapter 2

Types of Grasslands

Grasslands grow all around the world. There are two main types. Tropical grasslands called savannas grow near the **equator**. They are warm and have a rainy and a dry season.

Learn more here!

Temperate grasslands are farther away from the equator. They have some of the world's best soils. Cold winters provide most of the yearly **precipitation** as snow. The summers are hot.

Chapter 3

Grassland Plants

Forests cannot grow on grasslands. There is not enough rain. The most important plants in these biomes are grasses and shrubs. They can grow back quickly after wildfires.

Wildfires help prevent trees from taking over grasslands.

Learn more here!

Elephants stomp down bushes and trees when they move around savannas in Africa.

Short and tall grasses like lemon grass grow in savannas. Large, **grazing mammals**, like elephants, keep too many trees from growing. Frequent fires also prevent trees and shrubs from taking over.

Meadow grass and purple needlegrass cover the ground in **temperate**

grasslands. Wildflowers grow there too. They make great food for **pollinators**.

butterfly

The colors, shapes, and scents of flowers attract pollinators to them.

Chapter 4

Grassland Animals

Savannas are home to many amazing animals. Zebras and antelope move in large groups eating the grasses. They are hunted by lions and cheetahs. Kangaroos live in Australian savannas.

Complete an activity here!

19

Rodents and insects can burrow underground. This helps them survive any wildfires.

Temperate grasslands have lots of insects. Prairie dogs and gophers make their homes underground. Herds of bison live here. They keep the grasses short with the help of other **grazing** animals.

Making Connections

Text-to-Self

Would you rather see animals from tropical grasslands or temperate grasslands? Why?

Text-to-Text

Have you read a book about any other biomes? If so, how are they similar to and different from grasslands?

Text-to-World

Are wildfires good or bad for grasslands? Do you think the animals that live there are prepared to survive wildfires when they happen?

Glossary

climate – weather conditions that are usual in an area over a long period of time.

equator – an imaginary line around the middle of Earth, halfway between the north and south poles.

graze – to feed on plants like grasses.

mammal – an animal that makes milk to feed its young and usually has hair or fur on its skin.

pollinator – an animal that carries pollen from one part of a flower or plant to another.

precipitation – moisture such as rain, hail, or snow that falls to Earth.

temperate – having mild weather.

Index

animals, 4, 15–18, 21

plants, 4, 6–7, 12–18, 21

precipitation, 6–8, 11–12

savannas, 8, 14–15, 18

seasons, 8, 11

trees, 6–7, 13–15

tropical, 8

wildfire, 12–13, 20

Online Resources

popbooksonline.com

Thanks for reading this Cody Koala book!

Scan this code* and others like it in this book, or visit the website below to make this book pop!

popbooksonline.com/grassland-biome

*Scanning QR codes requires a web-enabled smart device with a QR code reader app and a camera.